7-day
detox

igloobooks

igloobooks

Published in 2016
by Igloo Books Ltd
Cottage Farm
Sywell
NN6 0BJ
www.igloobooks.com

Food photography and recipe development: © Stockfood, The Food Media Agency
Front cover images: © Stockfood, The Food Media Agency (top left and top right); iStock (main image and top middle)
Back inside flap: iStock

Designed by Stephen Jorgensen
Edited by Natalie Baker

LEO002 0316
4 6 8 10 9 7 5 3
ISBN 978-1-78557-012-4

Printed and manufactured in China

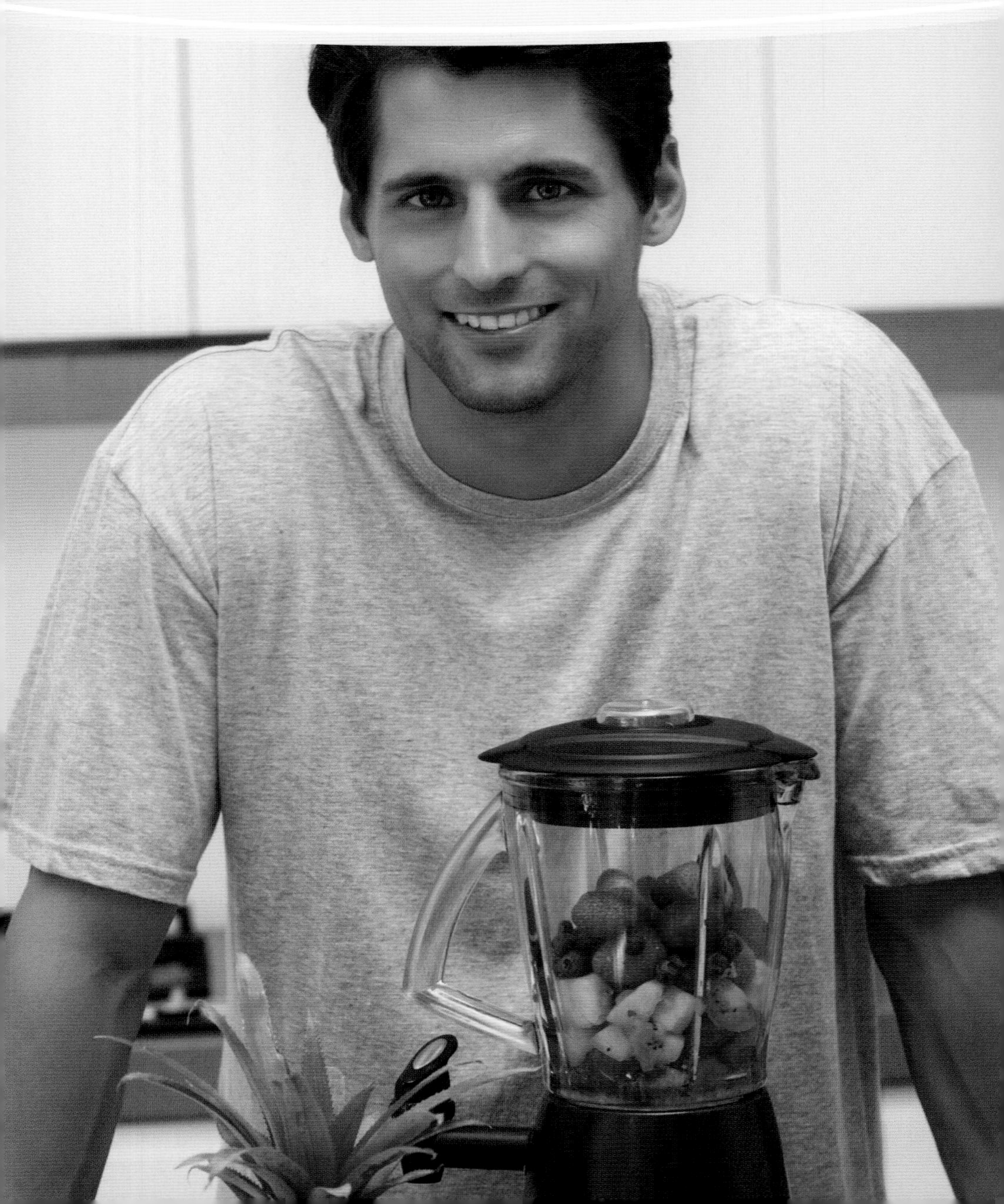

Contents

Who should detox?

Many health practitioners recommend that you detox at least once a year. However, some people shouldn't detox at all without seeking a doctor's advice first. If you are pregnant or breastfeeding, or if you have a chronic health condition, it may not be right for you. Speak to your GP before you start.

Introduction

Sometimes, you just don't feel at the top of your game. You may feel run down or a bit sluggish. Your brain might not be firing on all cylinders. Even though you're not actually ill, you've definitely lost that healthy glow. Sounds like it might be time for a detox!

What is detoxing?

Detoxing is a process that aims to cleanse the body of harmful toxins. In our daily lives we are constantly exposed to chemicals. They are in the air, in our food, in cleaning products and cosmetics, in furniture and appliances – in short, they are nearly everywhere.

Our bodies have efficient systems to get rid of toxins. The liver filters out impurities from the blood and the kidneys, intestines, lungs, lymph and skin also play a role. However, sometimes they need a bit of a hand. A detox programme can give your body's natural cleansing processes a boost.

Different ways to detox

There are so many different ways to detox that it can be confusing. Some programmes involve drinking only herbal teas and juices to cleanse your entire digestive system. Other programmes target specific toxins or areas of the body. Some people choose to fast for a few days, which means not eating and drinking only water or juice. Some popular 7-day detox regimes involve fasting on liquids for two days, followed by five days of a carefully chosen diet that will allow your digestive system to rest.

All About Detoxing

Detoxing is often in the news these days, but it isn't a new idea. In fact, traditional medicine in the Indian subcontinent has been promoting detoxing for thousands of years. This discipline is known as Ayurveda, which means the 'science of life', and emphasises moderation in many areas and focuses on keeping the body in balance.

Part of Ayurvedic medicine is 'panchakarma', which is a way of cleansing the body of toxins. It takes a holistic approach, focusing on both mind and body. The practice involves exercise, massage and the use of herbal remedies to keep the body in balance, boost spiritual and emotional growth, improve health and prevent diseases.

Detoxing in other cultures

You can find examples of detoxing in many ancient cultures. Before modern medicine was developed, many different peoples believed that good health was based on keeping the body in balance.

Sweating, fasting and the use of herbs played a role in the cleansing rituals of many different cultures. For example, some Native American tribes used sweat lodges – which are similar to saunas – as a way of religious cleansing.
The ancient Greeks and Romans also used sweat baths to keep healthy.
Fasting was used in many cultures as a means of spiritual and bodily purification.

The science of detox

In recent years, numerous scientific studies have tried to prove whether detox works or not. Depending on who you ask, you'll get a lot of different answers! However, most doctors, nutritionists and alternative health practitioners can agree on the health benefits of a diet based on fresh produce and wholegrains, with meat and dairy included sparingly and little or no use of refined sugar, caffeine, alcohol and tobacco.

Principles of Detoxing

Depending on which detox programme you choose, you'll be advised to eat a variety of different foods. Most detox diets are based around fresh fruit and vegetables, either eaten raw or in the form of juice. Juices are a good way to get the nutrients found in fruits and vegetables, without your digestive system having to work so hard to process them. Not all juices are equal: many contain a lot of added sugar, so check labels carefully. Making your own is a great way to avoid extra sugar.

What not to eat

Once you've done your juice fast, it's important to start re-introducing foods by choosing only the healthiest ones. This means saying 'no thanks' to milk and other dairy products, eggs and refined carbs such as white bread and biscuits. Lean meat and fish are healthy sources of protein, but you should avoid fatty meat, red meat and any kind of processed meat, such as sausages or cold cuts. Refined sugars are another big no-no.

What to eat

It may sound like nearly everything is prohibited, but there is a huge variety of healthy, delicious foods that you can eat on a detox. Nuts, seeds and pulses are a great source of energy. Healthy oils such as olive oil and flaxseed oil can replace butter. Wholegrains such as brown rice, quinoa and buckwheat make a great replacement for refined flour – and they're gluten-free, too!

The big picture

Doing a detox isn't just about changing what you eat. You need to try to reduce or eliminate your exposure to other types of toxins as well. Giving up alcohol and tobacco is an obvious first step, but what about the toxins found in cleaning products, as well as hair products and cosmetics? Look for natural alternatives that use plant-based ingredients and are paraben free.

Go organic!

One great way to detox your body is to choose organic food wherever it is available. To be certified as organic, fruits, vegetables and grains must be grown without the use of chemical fertilisers and there are strict rules on the use of pesticides as well. Even meat and dairy can be certified organic, if the animals are free-range and fed a diet that is as natural as possible. Organic farming is better for the environment and it's better for you, as it reduces your exposure to toxins.

Natural detoxifiers

Antioxidants are nutrients found in many fruits and vegetables that help neutralise harmful free radicals. An excess of free radicals in the body is thought to contribute to a number of health conditions such as cancer, heart disease, stroke and Alzheimer's disease. Consuming foods high in antioxidants, like blueberries, nuts, kale, sweet potatoes and green tea, may help to reduce the oxidative damage caused by these free radicals.

Other foods can help boost your digestive system. Citrus fruits such as oranges, limes and lemons have enzymes that will help cleanse the liver, so a warm glass of lemon water every day is a great idea. Foods such as garlic, mung beans, olive oil, asparagus, ginger and grapefruit also have positive effects. And of course, don't forget water. Drinking lots of water can help flush out toxins while keeping you hydrated.

Detox and de-stress

Being stressed triggers the release of certain hormones. These hormones can be useful, as they give you an 'adrenaline rush' that can help you through a difficult situation. However, if they build up in large amounts they can create toxins, so reducing stress is a key part of any detox regime. Activities such as meditation, mindfulness and yoga can help with this.

How Your Body Works

One of the main aims of a detox programme is to reduce stress on your liver and help boost its efficiency. This incredible organ filters the blood that comes from your digestive tract before sending it on to the rest of the body. This blood often contains nutrients, as well as alcohol, medications and toxins. The liver processes all these substances, storing some and detoxifying others. Some are passed back into the blood and others are sent to the large intestine to be eliminated. The liver also makes proteins that are important for blood clotting.

Liver problems

Not looking after your liver can have serious consequences. One of the most common liver problems is cirrhosis, which is often caused by drinking too much alcohol over a long period. Cirrhosis is the scarring that results from long-term damage and it prevents the liver from doing its job properly. Other problems include a build-up of fatty cells in the liver, which is more common in people who are obese, and hepatitis, which is an inflammation of the liver.

Helping your liver

The best way to keep your liver in good shape is to eat a healthy diet and exercise regularly. Alcohol can harm your liver, so drink it only in moderation. Watch out for the toxins in cleaning products, cigarettes, insecticides and aerosol products.

Let's hear it for the liver!

Your liver works very hard in terms of keeping you healthy. The average adult liver weighs between 1.2 and 1.5 kilograms, and it is reddish-brown in appearance. One of its most amazing features is that it can regenerate itself if part of it is removed! It is one of the few body parts that can do this.

Crucial kidneys

Your liver is definitely the big cheese when it comes to keeping your body toxin-free, but other organs play a role, too. Your kidneys filter blood to remove toxins and they also remove excess water. One of their main jobs is getting rid of urea, which is a toxin that is produced when the liver breaks down proteins. The kidneys transfer urea from the blood to the urine, which the body excretes.

If your kidneys aren't working properly, waste products and fluid can build up in your body, causing serious problems. You can look after your kidneys by drinking plenty of water – if your urine is any darker than straw-coloured, it's a sign that you may be dehydrated. Eating a healthy diet, avoiding cigarettes and alcohol, and maintaining a healthy weight and blood pressure also helps your kidneys.

The skin you're in

Your skin does a lot for you: it protects your body from external dangers, it helps to regulate your body temperature and contains the nerves that allow you to touch. But did you know that it also helps to eliminate toxins from the body? When we sweat, our bodies excrete ammonia, uric acid and urea.

The role of the gut

The intestines also have a role to play in ridding the body of toxins. The small intestine is mainly concerned with absorbing nutrients from food, but the large intestine helps get rid of waste. A diet rich in fibre helps the large intestine to work properly. The fibre binds with waste products in the gut and packages them up to be eliminated. Beans, wholegrains, lentils, dried fruit, fresh fruit and veg (the crunchier the better!), nuts and oats are all good sources of fibre.

Exercise and Stress Management

You've got your fridge stocked with organic fruit and veg and the cupboards are full of wholegrains and pulses. The juicer is standing ready and waiting on the kitchen work surface. You're ready to begin your detox, so it's time to get out the running shoes as well, right?

Wrong! Remember that detoxing is about cleansing and rebooting your body's systems, not losing weight. And you may get better results if you take a brief break from exercise. In fact, the amount of energy you'll get from juices probably won't be enough to fuel vigorous workouts.

Get your beauty sleep

You may find that you need less sleep at night during a detox, because your daytime activity levels are likely to be lower. However, you'll still need plenty of rest because your calorie intake will be lower than normal. Many detox experts recommend taking one or two short naps during the day. If you get enough rest, it will improve your results, since the body can focus its energy on healing instead of activity.

If you do decide to work out, take it easy and watch out for signs that you may be overdoing it. If you're getting dizzy and lightheaded when you exercise, or are in pain, stop what you're doing and talk to your GP if the symptoms continue.

Keep moving!

That's not to say that you should spend your detox period vegging on the sofa. Mild exercise stimulates the body's lymphatic system, which helps drain toxins out of the body. A brisk walk of about 20 minutes each day will keep things moving, and it won't use up too much of the energy that your body needs for the detox process. Swimming and cycling are also good options, if you take it easy.

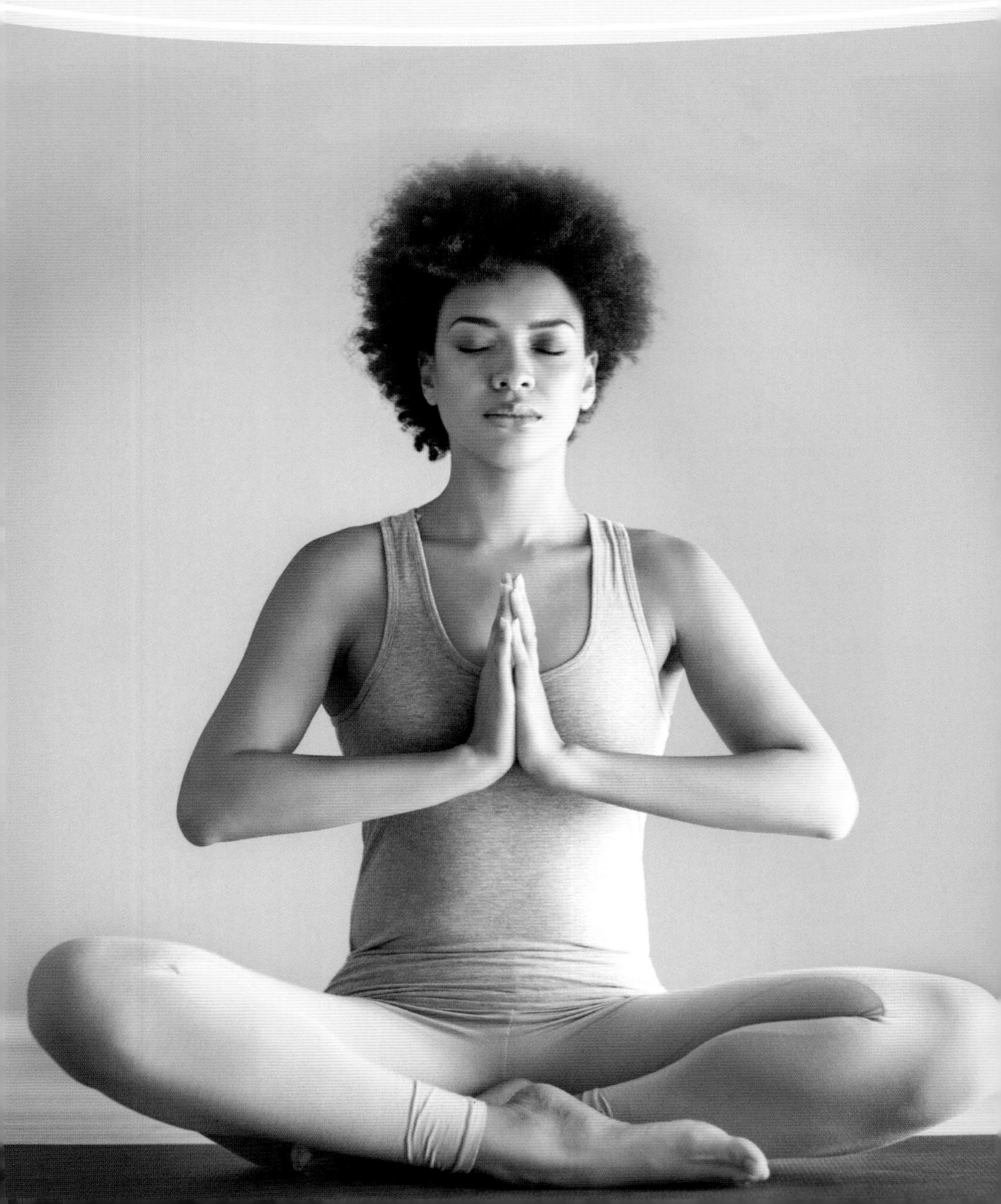

How to exercise

The best exercise options during a detox are those that gently stretch and stimulate the muscles, such as yoga and pilates. These disciplines can help improve strength, flexibility and muscle tone, in addition to helping to relax you. In fact, many health experts believe that some twisting yoga poses have a natural detoxifying effect. The motion can stimulate blood flow to organs such as the liver and kidneys, helping them to absorb nutrients and release toxins.

Yoga

Yoga is a great addition to any detox regime. This ancient form of exercise can boost both physical and mental well-being by focusing on strength, flexibility and breathing. Scientific studies have shown that it can help combat stress, as well as lowering blood pressure and reducing aches and pains.

Meditation and mindfulness

The practice of meditation and deep breathing can help restore balance to body and mind, take your mind off tiredness or hunger and help you keep focused on your goal of health and cleansing. Mindfulness is the practice of paying attention to the present moment, and it can reduce stress and improve your mood.

Have a bath!

A bath with Epsom salts will help you relax and de-stress, as well as eliminating toxins. Add a few scoops of Epsom salts to the bath and while you wait for it to fill, use a natural bristled brush and brush your skin with long strokes for a few minutes. This helps to open up your pores. Then have a lovely soak – about 20–30 minutes before bed is ideal. The Epsom salts will draw out excess sodium and other wastes from the body.

Get the Detox Glow

Once you get into your detox, you'll start to see positive results. If you're starting with a juice fast, it will help cleanse your digestive tract of unwanted waste.

When you give your digestive system a breather, it gives your liver and kidneys the chance to focus their efforts on filtering and purifying your blood. You'll feel better and you'll probably look better too. Those dark circles under your eyes should disappear and all that water you're drinking will help your skin to look clearer.

Cancel the cravings!

The first part of a detox is often the hardest, as our body craves the things it's no longer getting: sugar, caffeine, nicotine, alcohol, simple carbs, the list goes on and on. However, there is light at the end of the tunnel. As your body adjusts to living without these substances, the cravings for these foods will decrease.

Mental benefits

You might find that you feel mentally clearer and more focused during a detox. Meditation and mindfulness (see page 21) are part of the reason for this, but you're also helping your brain by reducing your dependence on stimulants such as caffeine, sugar and food additives. Taking a week from our busy lives to concentrate on looking after our body can have mental benefits, as well as physical ones.

Detox side effects

Any changes to your normal diet or routine can have side effects. During a detox, you may experience headaches or tiredness, cold sores or changes in bowel movements. You also may notice bad breath or body odour as your body gets rid of toxins. See a doctor if you are concerned about any of these symptoms, or if they don't improve once your detox is finished.

Keeping Motivated

Sticking to a detox regime can be hard, especially if you've never detoxed before. The fasting phase can leave you feeling tired and low at first, and when you re-introduce healthy foods you may get stressed about what to eat. Keeping motivated can be a big challenge!

Plan ahead

With a bit of prep work, you'll be able to get through the week and meet your goals. One good tip is to clear out your kitchen before you start, getting rid of any unhealthy processed foods that might tempt you. Another idea is to prepare some healthy meals in advance and then freeze them. If you reach a point where you're feeling tired, or just not motivated to cook, you'll have something nutritious that can easily be popped in the microwave or oven.

Reward yourself

Make a list of daily rewards for sticking with your detox programme. You may be used to treating yourself with chocolate, but think about non-food ways to keep yourself motivated. They could include a trip to the cinema or the farmers' market, a glossy magazine, a massage or a catch-up with a friend you haven't seen for a while. And the rewards shouldn't stop when the detox finishes. Keeping focused on your goals can help you to avoid relapsing into bad habits.

The more the merrier

One of the best ways to stay motivated throughout your detox is to have a friend or partner do it with you. If you work together, it's more likely that both of you will succeed. Even if they don't want to do the full detox, you should still share your plans with them. They can give you support and encouragement if you start to struggle, and congratulate you when you reach your goal.

Breakfasts and Brunches

Once you start re-introducing food as part of your detox programme, it's best to start each day with a healthy, nutritious breakfast. Most of us are used to eating toast, cereal or eggs at breakfast, so sticking to a detox diet usually means being adventurous in your food choices and trying something new.

If you have traditional tastes, how about porridge? Cook oats with unsweetened almond or soya milk and top with fresh fruit for a detox winner. Dairy-free yoghurt with a handful of berries on top provides useful antioxidants. Remember, there's no rule to say you can't eat vegetables for breakfast. The nutrients in asparagus make it a great choice. Quinoa and buckwheat are gluten-free grains that go well with vegetables and you can add chia or hemp seeds for a healthy kick.

Pumpkin Seed Milk Parfait

Serves: 4 / Preparation time: 10 minutes + overnight
Cooking time: 5 minutes / Calories per portion: 564

Ingredients

140 g / 5 oz / 1 ¼ cups pumpkin seeds

125 g / 4 ½ oz / ¾ cup rolled oats

1 tbsp coconut oil, melted

750 ml / 1 pint 6 fl. oz / 3 cups water, plus extra for soaking

1 tbsp agave nectar

100 g / 3 ½ oz / ⅔ cup unsulphured dried apricots, chopped

40 g / 1 ½ oz / ½ cup coconut flakes

125 g / 4 ½ oz / ¾ cup cherries, pitted and halved

2 tbsp goji berries

150 g / 5 oz / 1 cup strawberries, hulled and quartered

110 g / 4 oz / ½ cup unsweetened coconut milk yoghurt

4 sprigs of mint, to garnish

Method

1. Place 110 g / 4 oz / ¾ cup of the pumpkin seeds in a bowl and cover with cold water. Leave to soak overnight.

2. Preheat the grill to hot. Toss the oats with the coconut oil and spread out on a grilling tray. Toast under the grill for 1–2 minutes until golden all over. Remove to one side and leave to cool.

3. After soaking, drain the pumpkin seeds and place in a blender with the water and agave nectar. Blend on high until smooth. Strain through muslin into four serving mugs.

4. Add the apricots and coconut flakes and then top with a combination of the remaining ingredients, including the toasted oats and remaining pumpkin seeds.

5. Garnish with mint sprigs and serve immediately.

Blueberry Coconut Oatmeal

Serves: 4 / Preparation time: 5 minutes
Cooking time: 10 minutes / Calories per portion: 354

Ingredients

600 ml / 1 pint 2 fl. oz / 2 ½ cups unsweetened almond milk, plus extra to serve

200 ml / 7 fl. oz / ¾ cup light coconut milk

2 tbsp coconut sugar

150 g / 5 oz / 2 cups rolled oats

100 g / 3 ½ oz / ⅔ cup dried cherries

150 g / 5 oz / 1 cup blueberries

2 tbsp pecans, chopped

a few sprigs of mint, to garnish

Method

1. Combine the almond milk, coconut milk and coconut sugar in a saucepan. Warm over a moderate heat until boiling, stirring occasionally.

2. Add the oats, stir well and return to a boil. Reduce to a gentle simmer, then cook, stirring frequently for 3–4 minutes until the oatmeal has thickened. Stir through most of the cherries and about half of the blueberries.

3. Divide the oatmeal between serving bowls. Top with the remaining blueberries, cherries and the pecans.

4. Serve with extra almond milk and a garnish of mint sprigs.

Clean Green Juice

Serves: 4 / Preparation time: 5 minutes
Calories per portion: 39

Ingredients

1 medium cucumber, chopped

1 lime, juiced

1 tbsp light agave nectar

1 l / 1 pint 16 fl. oz / 4 cups water

55 g / 2 oz / 1 cup parsley, chopped

55 g / 2 oz / 1 cup coriander (cilantro), chopped

225 g / 8 oz / 1 cup crushed ice

Method

1. Combine the cucumber, lime juice, agave nectar and half of the water in a food processor or blender. Blend on high for 30 seconds.

2. Add the remaining ingredients, stir well and blend on high for a further 30 seconds until frothy.

3. Pour into glasses and serve immediately.

Chia Seed Pudding

Serves: 4 / Preparation time: 40 minutes + overnight
Calories per portion: 196

Ingredients

225 g / 8 oz / 1 ½ cups frozen mixed berries, thawed

2 tbsp lemon juice

2 tbsp light agave nectar

250 ml / 9 fl. oz / 1 cup unsweetened almond milk

225 g / 8 oz / 1 cup unsweetened coconut milk yoghurt

40 g / 1 ½ oz / ¼ cup chia seeds

a few sprigs of mint, to garnish

Method

1. Combine the thawed berries with the lemon juice and 1 tbsp of agave nectar in a food processor or blender. Blend on high until smooth.

2. Scrape into a bowl, cover and chill until ready to serve.

3. Whisk together the almond milk, yoghurt and remaining agave nectar in a mixing bowl. Add the chia seeds, whisk again briefly and leave to stand for 30 minutes.

4. After 30 minutes, stir the chia seed mixture, cover and chill overnight.

5. Give the chia seed pudding a quick stir and then divide between serving glasses. Top with the mixed berry purée and garnish with mint.

Muesli with Date Balls

Serves: 4 / Preparation time: 10 minutes
Cooking time: 20 minutes / Calories per portion: 565

Ingredients

160 g / 6 oz / 4 cups rolled oats

2 tbsp coconut sugar

non-fat cooking spray

75 g / 3 oz / 1 cup desiccated coconut

100 g / 3 ½ oz / ⅔ cup pitted dates

75 g / 3 oz / ¾ cup almonds, chopped

1 papaya, seeded and diced

150 g / 5 oz / 1 cup strawberries, hulled
and quartered

2 tbsp sugar and dairy-free dark chocolate
chunks

2 tbsp lemon juice

110 g / 4 oz / ⅔ cup raspberries, crushed

75 g / 3 oz / ½ cup blackberries

Method

1. Preheat the oven to 180°C (160°C fan) /
   350F / gas 4. Toss together the oats and
   coconut sugar in a bowl and then spritz
   with cooking spray. Spread out on a
   baking tray.

2. Bake for 15–18 minutes until crisp and
   starting to brown. Remove to a wire rack
   to cool.

3. Combine the coconut and pitted dates
   in a food processor and pulse on high
   for 2–3 minutes until smooth, pausing to
   scrape down the sides from time to time.

4. Scoop out tablespoons of the mixture and
   roll into balls between damp palms. Roll the
   balls in chopped almonds to coat evenly.

5. Toss the papaya, strawberries and
   chocolate chunks with the lemon juice.
   Divide between servings jars and top with
   the toasted muesli, crushed raspberries
   and blackberries. Serve with the date balls
   on the side.

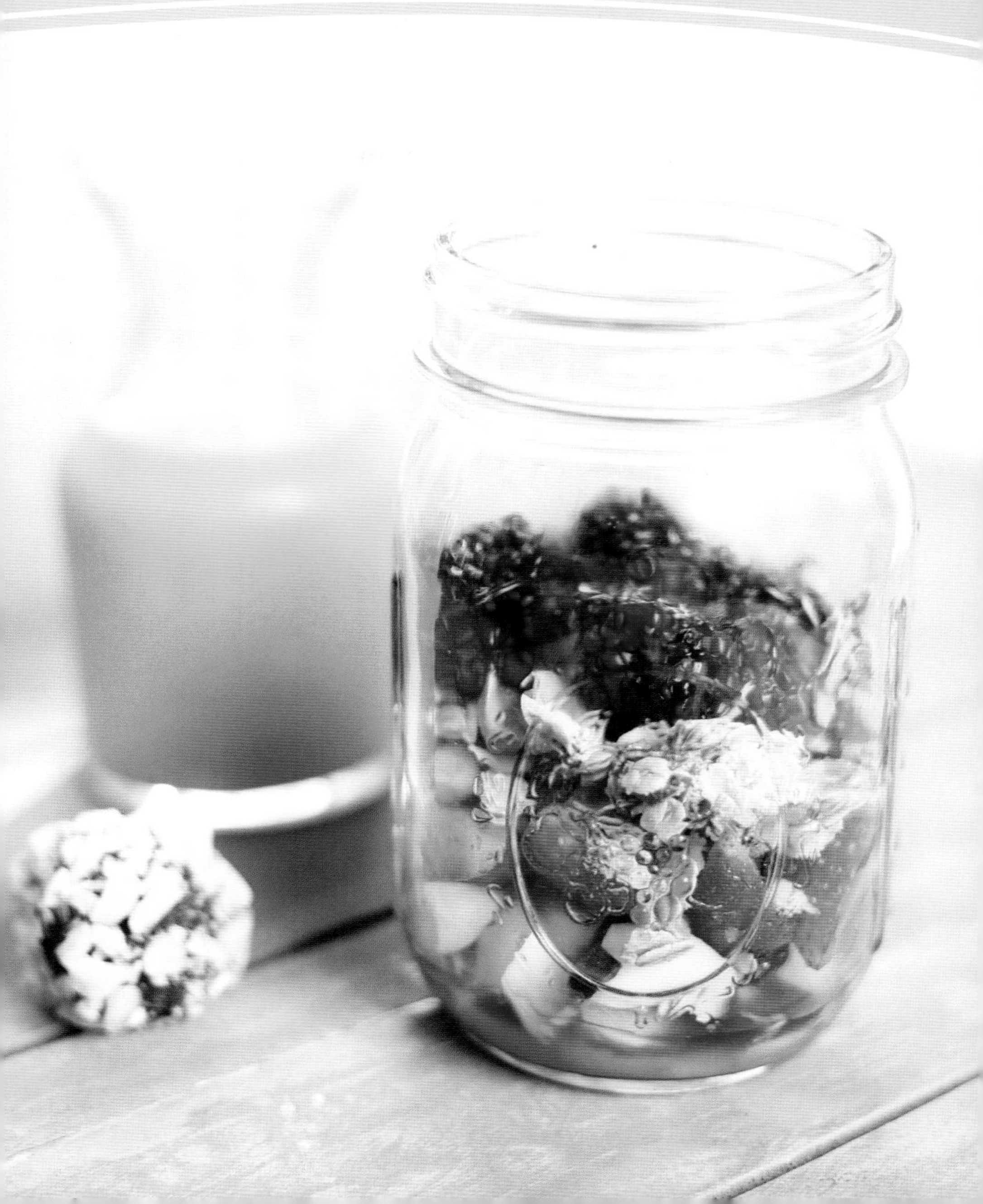

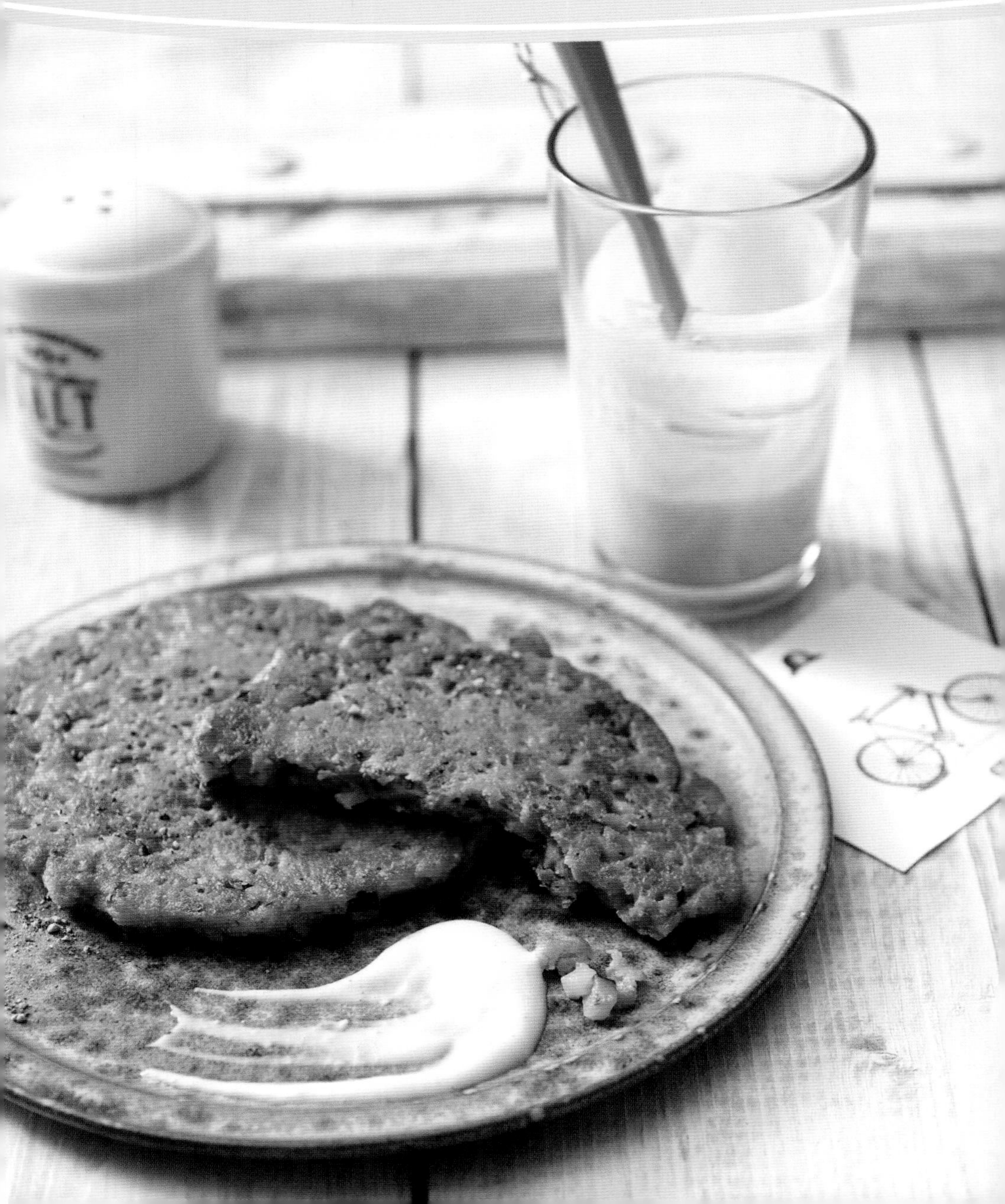

Chickpea Pancakes with Aioli

Serves: 4 / Preparation time: 10 minutes
Cooking time: 30 minutes / Calories per portion: 195

Ingredients

150 g / 5 oz / ⅔ cup silken tofu

1 small clove of garlic, minced

1 tsp Dijon mustard

1 tbsp lemon juice

150 g / 5 oz / 1 cup gram (chickpea) flour, sifted

½ tsp gluten-free baking powder

225 ml / 8 fl. oz / 1 cup unsweetened soy milk

½ large courgette (zucchini), finely diced

non-fat cooking spray

salt and freshly ground black pepper

Method

1. Combine the tofu, garlic, mustard, lemon juice and 100 ml / 3 ½ fl. oz / ½ cup of water in a food processor. Blend on high until smooth, then add a little water to achieve the consistency of a thick sauce. Season with salt and pepper, then chill.

2. Whisk together the gram flour, baking powder and seasoning in a mixing bowl. Add the soy milk gradually, whisking until a batter comes together. Stir through the courgette. Pour the batter into a jug and leave it to stand for 10 minutes.

3. Preheat a non-stick frying pan over a moderate heat until hot. Spray with non-fat cooking spray and pour a generous ladleful of the batter into the pan, letting it run to the sides.

4. Reduce the heat slightly and leave the pancake to cook for 2–3 minutes until golden underneath. Flip and cook the other side for a further 2 minutes.

5. Repeat this method for the remaining batter. Serve with the aioli.

Soy Yoghurt with Fruit Salad

Serves: 4 / Preparation time: 5 minutes
Calories per portion: 190

Ingredients

1 large Rocha pear, cored and diced

150 g / 5 oz / 1 cup blueberries

75 g / 3 oz / ½ cup green seedless grapes, halved

75 g / 3 oz / ½ cup blackberries

900 g / 2 lb / 4 cups unsweetened vanilla soy yoghurt

2 tbsp flaxseeds

Method

1. Arrange a little of the fruit in the base of four serving bowls.

2. Top with the soy yoghurt and then the remaining fruit.

3. Sprinkle over the flaxseeds and serve.

Light Bites and Lunches

Too often these days, we have lunch at our desks or on the go, eating whatever is convenient without taking the time to appreciate it. On a detox, you want to make every meal count. Focusing on having something healthy as well as appealing can turn lunchtime from a chore into the highlight of your day. Even a packed lunch can be exciting if you take the time to prepare something delicious!

When it comes to choosing a healthy lunch, salads are a no-brainer. Choose seasonal ingredients for a healthier salad. Add some toasted seeds or nuts to give it a bit of a crunch. Drizzling a bit of olive oil, lemon juice and balsamic vinegar is fine, but avoid sugar-laden dressings.

If you want something a bit more filling, vegetable-based soups are easy to make in advance and can be frozen in individual portions.

Creamy Pumpkin Soup

Serves: 4 / Preparation time: 15 minutes
Cooking time: 55 minutes / Calories per portion: 265

Ingredients

1.25 kg / 2 lb 12 oz / 7 cups pumpkin, cored and diced

2 tbsp olive oil

2 shallots, diced

2 cloves of garlic, minced

650 ml / 1 pint 4 fl. oz / 2 ⅔ cups vegetable stock

250 ml / 9 fl. oz / 1 cup light coconut milk

1 tbsp maple syrup

75 g / 3 oz / ⅓ cup unsweetened coconut milk yoghurt

2 tbsp chopped chives

salt and freshly ground black pepper

Method

1. Preheat the oven to 180°C (160°C fan) / 350F / gas 4. Toss the pumpkin with 1 tbsp of oil and some seasoning, then spread out on a baking tray.

2. Roast for 35–40 minutes until brown at the edges. Remove from the oven and set to one side.

3. Heat the remaining oil in a large saucepan set over a medium heat. Add the shallots and garlic, frying for 2–3 minutes.

4. Add the pumpkin, stock, coconut milk and maple syrup, stirring well. Cook until simmering, then transfer the contents of the pan to a blender.

5. Blend on high until smooth. Return the soup to the saucepan and warm over a medium heat, seasoning to taste with salt and pepper.

6. Ladle into bowls and serve with a swirl of coconut milk yoghurt and a garnish of chives and black pepper.

Trout Carpaccio with Beetroot Salsa

Serves: 4 / Preparation time: 40 minutes

Calories per portion: 233

Ingredients

450 g / 1 lb trout fillet, skinned and pin-boned

2 lemons, juiced

½ tsp dried oregano

300 g / 11 oz / 2 cups cooked beetroot, drained and diced

55 g / 2 oz / ⅓ cup baby capers, drained

1 shallot, finely chopped

2 tbsp rice wine vinegar

2 tbsp flat-leaf parsley, chopped

2 tbsp mint, chopped

30 g / 1 oz / ½ cup rocket (arugula)

2 tbsp extra-virgin olive oil

sea salt and freshly ground black pepper

Method

1. Thinly slice the trout fillet using a sharp chef's knife. Arrange the slices, overlapping slightly, on a serving plate. Dress with half the lemon juice and season with pepper and dried oregano. Cover and chill for 30 minutes.

2. Mix together the beetroot, capers, shallot, rice wine vinegar, remaining lemon juice, chopped herbs and seasoning in a large bowl. Cover and set to one side.

3. Once the trout has marinated for 30 minutes, remove it from the fridge and top with some of the beetroot salsa.

4. Garnish with rocket leaves, a drizzle of olive oil and some sea salt and serve with the remaining salsa on the side.

Rainbow Salad

Serves: 4 / Preparation time: 10 minutes
Calories per portion: 274

Ingredients

2 tbsp rice wine vinegar

1 tsp Dijon mustard

110 ml / 4 fl. oz / ½ cup avocado oil

1 small red cabbage, shredded

225 g / 8 oz / 4 cups curly kale, chopped

2 carrots, grated

225 g / 8 oz / 1 ½ cups broad (fava) beans, shelled

1 red pepper, diced

1 yellow pepper, diced

a bunch of coriander (cilantro), leaves picked

75 g / 3 oz / ¾ cup cashews

salt and freshly ground black pepper

Method

1. Whisk together the vinegar, mustard and seasoning in a mixing bowl. Add the avocado oil in a slow, steady stream, whisking until the dressing has emulsified.

2. Mix together the cabbage, kale, carrots, broad beans and peppers in a large mixing bowl. Add the dressing, toss well and lift the salad into bowls.

3. Top with coriander leaves and cashews before serving.

Tofu Seaweed Salad

Serves: 4 / Preparation time: 15 minutes
Calories per portion: 305

Ingredients

2 tbsp rice wine vinegar

1 tbsp almond butter

110 ml / 4 fl. oz / ½ cup avocado oil

300 g / 11 oz / 2 cups firm tofu, cubed

55 g / 2 oz / ⅓ cup black sesame seeds

55 g / 2 oz / ⅓ cup white sesame seeds

110 g / 4 oz / 2 cups pink laver seaweed,
roughly chopped

150 g / 5 oz / 3 cups wakame seaweed,
roughly chopped

salt and freshly ground black pepper

Method

1. Whisk together the rice wine vinegar,
almond butter and seasoning in a small
mixing bowl. Whisk in the oil in a slow,
steady stream until the dressing has
emulsified.

2. Roll the cubes of tofu in the sesame
seeds, pressing them gently into the
seeds to adhere.

3. Toss the two seaweeds with the dressing
and arrange with the tofu cubes in bowls.

Celeriac and Spinach Soup

Serves: 4 / Preparation time: 10 minutes
Cooking time: 40 minutes / Calories per portion: 125

Ingredients

120 g / 4 oz / 2 cups curly kale, chopped

2 tbsp avocado oil

2 cloves of garlic, minced

1 onion, finely chopped

1 medium celeriac, peeled and diced

750 ml / 1 pint 6 fl. oz / 3 cups
   vegetable stock

225 g / 8 oz / 5 cups baby spinach, washed

100 g / 3 ½ oz / ½ cup unsweetened
   coconut milk yoghurt

1 lemon

salt and freshly ground black pepper

Method

1. Preheat the oven to 180°C (160°C fan) /
   350F / gas mark 4. Spread the kale out
   on a baking tray and season with salt
   and pepper.

2. Bake for 12–15 minutes until dry and crisp
   at the edges. Remove to a wire rack.

3. Heat the oil in a large saucepan set over
   a medium heat until hot. Add the garlic,
   onion and celeriac and fry for 3 minutes,
   stirring frequently. Add the stock, stir well
   and cook until simmering.

4. Simmer for 8–10 minutes until the celeriac
   is very tender. Stir in the spinach and
   yoghurt and then blend in a food processor
   until smooth.

5. Return the soup to the saucepan and warm
   over a low heat. Season to taste with salt
   and pepper. Cut half the lemon into slices
   and reserve the other half.

6. Ladle the soup into bowls and top with kale
   chips, lemon slices, a squeeze of lemon
   juice and sunflower seeds.

Gluten-free Falafel

Serves: 4 / Preparation time: 20 minutes
Cooking time: 15 minutes / Calories per portion: 332

Ingredients

650 g / 1 lb 7 oz / 3 cups canned chickpeas (garbanzo beans), rinsed and drained

3 cloves of garlic, chopped

1 ½ tbsp tahini

¼ tsp ground cumin

55 ml / 2 fl. oz / ¼ cup avocado oil

55 g / 2 oz / ⅓ cup gram (chickpea) flour, plus extra if needed

1 lemon, cut into wedges

a small bunch of mint

225 g / 8 oz / 1 cup unsweetened almond milk yoghurt

salt and freshly ground black pepper

Method

1. Preheat the oven to 180°C (160°C fan) / 350F / gas mark 4. Line a baking tray with greaseproof paper.

2. Combine the chickpeas, garlic, tahini, cumin, 2 tbsp of oil and some seasoning in a food processor. Blend on high until the mixture is smooth.

3. Scrape the mixture into a bowl and stir in the gram flour, one tablespoon at a time, until the mixture is thick. Season to taste with some lemon juice and seasoning.

4. Shape into quenelles using two tablespoons and arrange on the prepared baking tray, spaced apart. Drizzle with the remaining oil.

5. Bake for 12–15 minutes, turning them halfway through, until golden brown. Remove to a wire rack to cool.

6. Finely chop some mint leaves and whisk with the yoghurt and a squeeze of lemon juice. Season and grate over fresh lemon zest, serving with a garnish of mint.

Beetroot and Orange Salad

Serves: 4 / Preparation time: 20 minutes
Calories per portion: 329

Ingredients

300 g / 11 oz / 2 cups cooked beetroot
  in vinegar, diced

2 blood oranges, peeled, pith removed
  and segmented

2 tbsp rice wine vinegar

75 g / 3 oz / ¾ cup walnut halves,
  roughly chopped

¼ wholemeal sourdough loaf,
  cut into croutons

a small bunch of thyme

salt and freshly ground black pepper

Method

1. Toss together the beetroot, sliced oranges,
   rice wine vinegar and seasoning in a mixing
   bowl. Cover and chill for 15 minutes.

2. Remove from the fridge after chilling and
   stir through the walnuts and croutons.

3. Adjust the seasoning to taste and serve
   with a garnish of thyme on plates.

Main Meals

After sticking to your detox regime for breakfast and lunch, you deserve a treat. It's time to cook a delicious dinner made from fresh ingredients that are both tasty and good for you. The recipes in this section will give you loads of ideas for appealing meals that are easy to prepare.

If you're eating salads for lunch, dinner is a good time to get your protein requirements. Avoid red meat and stick to lean cuts, such as grilled chicken breast or fish. You should aim to get a decent proportion of your protein needs from pulses such as chickpeas, beans or lentils.

Or why not try making vegetables the star of the show? Eating vegetarian can be better for your health and it's better for the planet, too. Roasted squash can be made into casseroles and vegetarian chilli is both warming and nutritious. Aubergines are great with roasted tomatoes and garlic. If you're craving starchy foods to accompany your meal, stick to gluten-free or wholegrain versions, such as brown rice, quinoa, buckwheat or wholegrain pasta.

Sea Bass with Samphire

Serves: 4 / Preparation time: 15 minutes

Cooking time: 15 minutes / Calories per portion: 401

Ingredients

225 g / 8 oz / 1 ½ cups Charlotte potatoes, peeled and turned

75 ml / 3 fl. oz / ⅓ cup olive oil

400 g / 14 oz sea bass fillets, pin-boned

8 scallops, roe removed

225 g / 8 oz / 4 cups samphire, washed

150 ml / 5 fl. oz / ⅔ cup unsweetened soy milk

2 tbsp black poppy seeds

30 g / 1 oz / 1 cup cress

1 tbsp avocado oil

salt and freshly ground black pepper

Method

1. Cook the potatoes in a large saucepan of salted, boiling water for 10–12 minutes.

2. Meanwhile, heat 2 tbsp of olive oil in a large sauté pan set over a medium heat. Season the sea bass fillets and lay in the oil, skin-side down.

3. Fry, undisturbed, for 4–5 minutes until the skin is crisp and golden, then flip. Season the scallops and add them to the pan. Cook both for 2 minutes, flipping the scallops after 1 minute.

4. Remove the fish and scallops from the pan to a plate and cover. Add the samphire and a splash of water to the pan, cover and steam for 3 minutes until tender.

5. Whisk together the remaining oil with the soy milk, poppy seeds and seasoning. Add it to the samphire and warm through for 1–2 minutes.

6. Drain the potatoes. Spoon the samphire and sauce onto plates. Serve with the remaining ingredients and a drizzle of oil.

Cod with Radish Salad

Serves: 4 / Preparation time: 10 minutes
Cooking time: 10 minutes / Calories per portion: 198

Ingredients

600 g / 1 lb 5 oz skinless cod fillet pieces, pin-boned

55 ml / 2 fl. oz / ¼ cup avocado oil

2 tbsp chives, chopped

225 g / 8 oz / 1 ½ cups mixed assorted radishes, sliced

1 large carrot, thinly sliced

2 tbsp lemon juice

a small bunch of coriander (cilantro), leaves picked

a few sprigs of thyme

1 tbsp edible flowers (optional)

flaked sea salt

freshly ground black pepper

Method

1. Preheat the grill to high. Rub the cod fillet with 2 tbsp of oil and position on a grilling tray. Season with salt and pepper and top with a few chives.

2. Grill for 4–5 minutes, turning occasionally, until the cod is golden and flaking easily.

3. Meanwhile, mix together the radishes, carrot, lemon juice, herbs, remaining oil, edible flowers if using and seasoning in a mixing bowl to make a quick salad.

4. Remove the cod from the grill and lift it onto platters. Top with the carrot and radish salad and serve immediately.

Courgette Spaghetti

Serves: 4 / Preparation time: 20 minutes
Cooking time: 5 minutes / Calories per portion: 266

Ingredients

300 g / 11 oz / 2 cups cherry tomatoes, halved

55 ml / 2 fl. oz / ¼ cup sherry vinegar

a few sprigs of thyme, torn

55 ml / 2 fl. oz / ¼ cup avocado oil

2 large courgettes (zucchinis), washed

2 medium carrots, peeled

110 g / 4 oz / 1 cup pine nuts

salt and freshly ground black pepper

Method

1. Toss together the cherry tomatoes, sherry vinegar, thyme, seasoning and half the oil in a mixing bowl. Cover and set to one side.

2. Using a spiralizer, turn the courgettes and carrots through the machine to create spaghetti-like strands of vegetable.

3. Soak the vegetable spaghetti in cold water and then drain and pat dry. Toss with the remaining oil and season to taste with salt and pepper.

4. Toast the pine nuts in a dry frying pan set over moderate heat until lightly golden. Remove the nuts from the pan.

5. Serve the vegetable spaghetti with the cherry tomato salad and pine nuts on top.

Pumpkin Curry

Serves: 4 / Preparation time: 10 minutes

Cooking time: 30 minutes / Calories per portion: 299

Ingredients

1 onion, chopped

4 cloves of garlic

2 tsp ground coriander

2 tsp Madras curry powder

a pinch of coconut sugar

2 tbsp coconut oil

1 tsp cumin seeds

900 g / 2 lb / 8 cups sugarloaf pumpkin, cored and diced

175 g / 6 oz / 1 cup brown basmati rice, rinsed in several changes of water

500 ml / 18 fl. oz / 2 cups vegetable stock

salt and freshly ground black pepper

Method

1. Blitz together the onion, garlic, ground coriander, curry powder, coconut sugar, seasoning and a splash of warm water in a food processor until smooth.

2. Heat the oil in a saucepan set over a medium heat until hot. Add the cumin seeds and fry for 30 seconds.

3. Add the onion paste, fry for 2 minutes and then stir in the pumpkin and rice. Cover with the stock, stir well and cook until simmering.

4. Cover the saucepan with a lid and cook over a reduced heat for 10–12 minutes until the rice and pumpkin are tender.

5. Remove the saucepan from the heat and let the rice and pumpkin stand covered for 10 minutes.

6. Fluff with a fork, season to taste and spoon into bowls before serving.

Carrot Beetroot Pancakes

Serves: 4 / Preparation time: 10 minutes
Cooking time: 20 minutes / Calories per portion: 315

Ingredients

125 ml / 4 ½ fl. oz / ½ cup red wine vinegar

300 g / 11 oz / 2 cups beetroot in vinegar, drained and cut into batons

1 large red onion, finely sliced

150 g / 5 oz / 1 cup oat flour

1 ½ tsp gluten-free baking powder

225 ml / 8 fl. oz / 1 cup unsweetened almond milk

55 ml / 2 fl. oz / ¼ cup avocado oil

75 g / 3 oz / ¾ cup carrot, finely grated

1 tbsp black poppy seeds

2 sprigs of mint, to garnish

225 g / 8 oz / 1 cup unsweetened coconut milk yoghurt

1 lemon

sea salt

Method

1. Warm the red wine vinegar with 125 ml / 4 fl. oz / ½ cup of water in a saucepan. Add the beetroot and red onion, stirring well. Cover with a lid and set to one side.

2. Combine the oat flour, baking powder and a pinch of salt in a bowl. Whisk in the milk and 2 tbsp of oil until a batter forms. Fold through the grated carrot and poppy seeds.

3. Heat 1 tsp of the remaining oil in a non-stick frying pan. Cook small ladles of the batter in the pan until golden and set. Flip and cook the other side for a further minute. Repeat this method, using fresh oil for each one. Finely slice some mint leaves and set them to one side.

4. Fill the pancakes with the beetroot and red onion and fold over in half. Lift onto plates and top with yoghurt, sliced mint leaves and grate over some lemon zest.

5. Serve with the remaining yoghurt on the side, along with lemon slices and mint sprigs to garnish.

Quinoa Broccoli Salad

Serves: 4 / Preparation time: 10 minutes
Cooking time: 25 minutes / Calories per portion: 461

Ingredients

175 g / 6 oz / 1 cup quinoa, rinsed

2 large, skinless chicken breasts, sliced

3 tbsp avocado oil

400 g / 14 oz / 3 ½ cups tenderstem broccoli, trimmed

400 g / 14 oz / 2 ⅔ cups cooked beetroot, cut into wedges

75 g / 3 oz / ¾ cup pine nuts

½ lemon, juiced

salt and freshly ground black pepper

Method

1. Place the quinoa in a saucepan set over a moderate heat. Toast the quinoa until dry and then cover with 500 ml / 18 fl. oz / 2 cups of water. Cook until boiling, then cover with a lid and cook over a reduced heat for 15 minutes.

2. Preheat the grill to hot. Toss the chicken with the oil and seasoning and then arrange on a grilling tray.

3. Grill for 8–10 minutes, turning occasionally, until golden and cooked through.

4. Meanwhile, steam the broccoli over a saucepan of simmering water for 5–7 minutes until tender.

5. Once the quinoa is ready, remove it to one side and leave it to stand covered for 5 minutes. Fluff with a fork, then add the broccoli, chicken, beetroot, pine nuts, lemon juice and seasoning.

6. Toss well and spoon into serving bowls.

Creamy Asparagus Curry

Serves: 4 / Preparation time: 10 minutes

Cooking time: 20 minutes / Calories per portion: 412

Ingredients

2 tbsp avocado oil

2 tbsp curry paste

450 g / 1 lb / 3 cups floury potatoes, peeled and diced

600 ml / 1 pint 6 fl. oz / 2 ½ cups unsweetened light coconut milk

275 g / 10 oz / 2 ½ cups green asparagus, trimmed and chopped

75 g / 3 oz / ¾ cup unsalted peanuts

1 tbsp fish sauce

1 tbsp rice wine vinegar

a bunch of coriander (cilantro), roughly torn

a bunch of Thai basil, leaves picked

salt and freshly ground black pepper

Method

1. Heat the oil in a saucepan set over a moderate heat until hot. Add the curry paste and fry for 1 minute.

2. Add the potato, stir well and fry for a further minute. Cover with the coconut milk and 250 ml / 9 fl. oz / 1 cup of water and cook until simmering.

3. Simmer for 10 minutes until the potato is tender. Add the asparagus, peanuts, fish sauce and vinegar and cook for a further 3 minutes.

4. Season to taste with salt and pepper. Ladle into bowls and serve with a garnish of herbs on the side.

Prawn Skewers with Noodles

Serves: 4 / Preparation time: 10 minutes
Cooking time: 15 minutes / Calories per portion: 375

Ingredients

225 g / 8 oz / 2 cups fine rice noodles

3 tbsp sesame oil

12 prawns (shrimp), peeled with
  heads removed

a large handful of Thai basil leaves

2 stalks of celery, finely sliced

2 spring onions (scallions), finely sliced

150 g / 5 oz / 1 cup cherry tomatoes, halved

2 tbsp rice wine vinegar

1 tbsp fish sauce

1 tbsp tamari soy sauce

a small bunch of coriander (cilantro),
  chopped

4 thin bamboo skewers

Method

1. Place the noodles and 1 tbsp of sesame
   oil in a large, heatproof bowl. Cover with
   boiling water, stir gently and leave to soften
   for 10 minutes.

2. Meanwhile, preheat the grill to hot.
   Thread three prawns onto each bamboo
   skewer, interspersed with basil leaves.
   Brush with more sesame oil and season
   with salt and pepper.

3. Arrange on a grilling tray and grill for
   4 minutes, turning once, until pink and
   tender. Remove from the grill and set to
   one side.

4. Drain the noodles and toss with the
   celery, spring onions, cherry tomatoes,
   rice wine vinegar, fish sauce, soy sauce
   and coriander.

5. Lift the noodle salad into bowls and serve
   with the prawn skewers on the side.

Desserts

Think of a dessert and you'll probably think of something made with cream, eggs or sugar. The truth is that most of the desserts we eat are no good for a detox diet. You don't need to give up sweets entirely – you just need to rethink what dessert is! It's also good to change it from a daily ritual to a once-or-twice-a-week treat.

Fresh fruit makes a great dessert; its natural sweetness can satisfy cravings and many fruits are loaded with antioxidants. Mix with dairy-free yoghurt and nuts or seeds to make a delicious, creamy parfait. You can even turn fruit into a healthy crumble by replacing the traditional topping ingredients with oats, ground nuts and gluten-free flours.

If you like to bake, why not try some new ingredients? Plain (all-purpose) flour can often be replaced with healthier flours, such as buckwheat or brown rice flour. Substitute sugar for natural sweeteners such as puréed apple, stevia or maple syrup. Herbs and spices such as ginger, cinnamon or mint can give your recipes a delicious twist.

Yoghurt with Raspberry Coulis

Serves: 4 / Preparation time: 10 minutes
Cooking time: 15 minutes / Calories per portion: 407

Ingredients

225 g / 8 oz / 1 ½ cups raspberries

½ lemon, juiced

2 tbsp agave nectar

450 g / 1 lb / 2 cups unsweetened soy milk yoghurt

450 g / 1 lb / 2 cups unsweetened coconut milk yoghurt

100 g / 3 ½ oz / 1 cup hazelnuts (cobnuts), chopped

a pinch of ground cinnamon

Method

1. Combine the raspberries, lemon juice, agave nectar and 2 tbsp of water in a saucepan.

2. Cook over a low heat, stirring occasionally, until the raspberries are soft and juicy. Purée in a food processor or blender until smooth.

3. Pass the purée through a fine sieve into a bowl. Cover and chill until needed.

4. Mix together the two yoghurts and divide between four serving cups or pots.

5. Toast the chopped hazelnuts with a pinch of ground cinnamon in a dry frying pan set over a medium heat. Once the nuts are aromatic and golden, remove from the pan and leave them to cool slightly.

6. Top the yoghurt with raspberry coulis and chopped hazelnuts before serving.

Cucumber Mint Sorbet

Serves: 4 / Preparation time: 10 minutes + 4 ½ hours
Cooking time: 5 minutes / Calories per portion: 101

Ingredients

a small bunch of mint
1 lime, juiced
175 ml / 6 fl. oz / ¾ cup water
75 g / 3 oz / ½ cup agave nectar
300 g / 11 oz / 3 cups cucumber, chopped
2 tsp pink peppercorns
2 tbsp pecans, roughly chopped

Method

1. Pick a small handful of mint leaves and roughly chop. Combine them with the lime juice, water and agave nectar in a small saucepan.

2. Cook over a moderate heat, stirring occasionally, until boiling. Remove from the heat and leave it to cool slightly.

3. Blitz the cucumber in a food processor until smooth. Add the syrup and blitz again until smooth. Stir in the peppercorns.

4. Churn the mixture in an ice cream machine according to the manufacturer's instructions. Once soft and frozen, scoop into a freezable container and freeze for at least 4 hours.

5. Remove the sorbet 10 minutes before serving. Scoop out and serve with a garnish of mint leaves and pecans.

Coconut, Date and Cacao Bars

Makes: 12 pieces / Preparation time: 25 minutes + setting
Calories per portion: 240

Ingredients

225 g / 8 oz / 1 ½ cups pitted medjool dates

150 g / 5 oz / 4 cups desiccated coconut

75 g / 3 oz / ½ cup cacao powder, sifted

110 g / 4 oz / 1 cup pecans

75 g / 3 oz / ⅓ cup dark agave nectar

110 ml / 4 fl. oz / ½ cup unsweetened
almond milk

75 ml / 3 fl. oz / ⅓ cup coconut oil, melted

a pinch of salt

Method

1. Place the dates in a large heatproof bowl and cover with boiling water. Leave them to soak for 15 minutes.

2. In the meantime, grease and line a 20 cm (8 in) square baking tin with greaseproof paper.

3. Drain the dates and place in a food processor along with the remaining ingredients, saving 2 tbsp of desiccated coconut for a garnish. Pulse until the mixture comes together.

4. Press the mixture into the prepared tin and top with the remaining desiccated coconut. Leave to set at room temperature.

5. Once set, turn out carefully and cut into portions before serving.

Iced Kiwi Soup

Serves: 4 / Preparation time: 10 minutes + 2 hours
Cooking time: 10 minutes / Calories per portion: 146

Ingredients

400 g / 14 oz / 2 ⅔ cups red gooseberries, washed (use white if not available)

75 g / 3 oz / ⅓ cup light agave nectar

a few drops of vanilla extract

4 kiwi fruit, peeled and diced

a small bunch of mint, leaves picked

250 ml / 9 fl. oz / 1 cup unsweetened almond milk

Method

1. Combine the gooseberries, agave nectar and vanilla extract with 2 tbsp of water in a saucepan.

2. Cook over a low heat, stirring occasionally, until the gooseberries are softened and starting to break down.

3. Add 1 l / 2 pints 1 fl. oz / 4 ¼ cups of iced water to the saucepan, stir well and pour everything into a bowl. Add the kiwi, a few torn mint leaves and the almond milk, stirring again.

4. Cover and chill for 2 hours until cold.

5. Ladle into bowls and serve with a garnish of chopped and whole mint leaves.

Coconut Cacao Smoothie

Serves: 4 / Preparation time: 5 minutes
Cooking time: 10 minutes / Calories per portion: 282

Ingredients

55 g / 2 oz / ⅓ cup cacao powder

2 tbsp almond butter

400 ml / 14 fl. oz / 1 ⅔ cups light unsweetened coconut milk

600 ml / 1 pint 2 fl oz / 2 ½ cups unsweetened almond milk

55 g / 2 oz / ¼ cup light agave nectar

80 g / 3 oz / 2 cups rolled oats

1 tbsp naturally sweetened dark chocolate, grated

Method

1. Combine the cacao powder, almond butter and a little of the coconut milk in a saucepan. Whisk briefly to make a paste, then whisk in the remaining coconut milk and the almond milk.

2. Add the agave nectar and warm the mixture over a medium heat, stirring occasionally, until it starts to simmer.

3. Pour into a food processor, add most of the oats and blend on high until smooth. Pour back into the saucepan and return to a simmer.

4. Pour into mugs and garnish with the remaining oats and grated chocolate on top.

Date Energy Balls

Makes: approx. 28 balls / Preparation time: 15 minutes
Calories per portion: 97

Ingredients

110 g / 4 oz / 1 cup almonds
110 g / 4 oz / 1 cup walnuts
150 g / 5 oz / 1 cup raisins
150 g / 5 oz / 1 cup medjool dates, pitted
2 tbsp hot water
¼ tsp ground cinnamon
½ tsp vanilla extract
75 g / 3 oz / ¾ cup white sesame seeds

Method

1. Combine all the ingredients apart from the sesame seeds in a food processor. Pulse until the mixture comes together.

2. Scoop out scant tablespoons of the mixture and roll into balls between slightly damp palms.

3. Roll half of the balls in sesame seeds to coat.

4. Leave to set briefly before serving.

Maple Cacao Brownies

Makes: 12 squares / Preparation time: 15 minutes
Cooking time: 45 minutes / Calories per portion: 183

Ingredients

175 g / 6 oz / 1 ¼ cups gram (chickpea) flour
75 g / 3 oz / ½ cup raw cacao powder
1 tsp gluten-free baking powder
a pinch of salt
150 g / 5 oz / ⅔ cup maple syrup
110 g / 4 oz / ½ cup unsweetened
   apple sauce
55 ml / 2 fl. oz / ¼ cup unsweetened
   almond milk
55 ml / 2 fl. oz / ¼ cup coconut oil
1 tsp vanilla extract
100 g / 3 ½ oz / ⅔ cup naturally sweetened
   vegan chocolate chips

Method

1. Preheat the oven to 180°C (160°C fan)
   / 350F / gas mark 4. Grease and line a
   deep 30 x 18 cm (12 x 7 in) baking tin with
   greaseproof paper.

2. Combine the flour, cacao powder, baking
   powder and a pinch of salt in a large mixing
   bowl. Whisk together the maple syrup,
   apple sauce, almond milk, coconut oil
   and vanilla extract in a mixing jug.

3. Add the wet ingredients into the dry,
   folding to combine with a spatula. Melt the
   chocolate chips in a microwaveable bowl
   for 30 second intervals on high. Let the
   melted chocolate chips cool slightly before
   folding into the batter.

4. Scrape the batter into the prepared tin and
   bake for 35–40 minutes until a cake tester
   comes out just clean from the centre of
   the brownie.

5. Remove to a wire rack to cool. Cut into
   portions and serve.

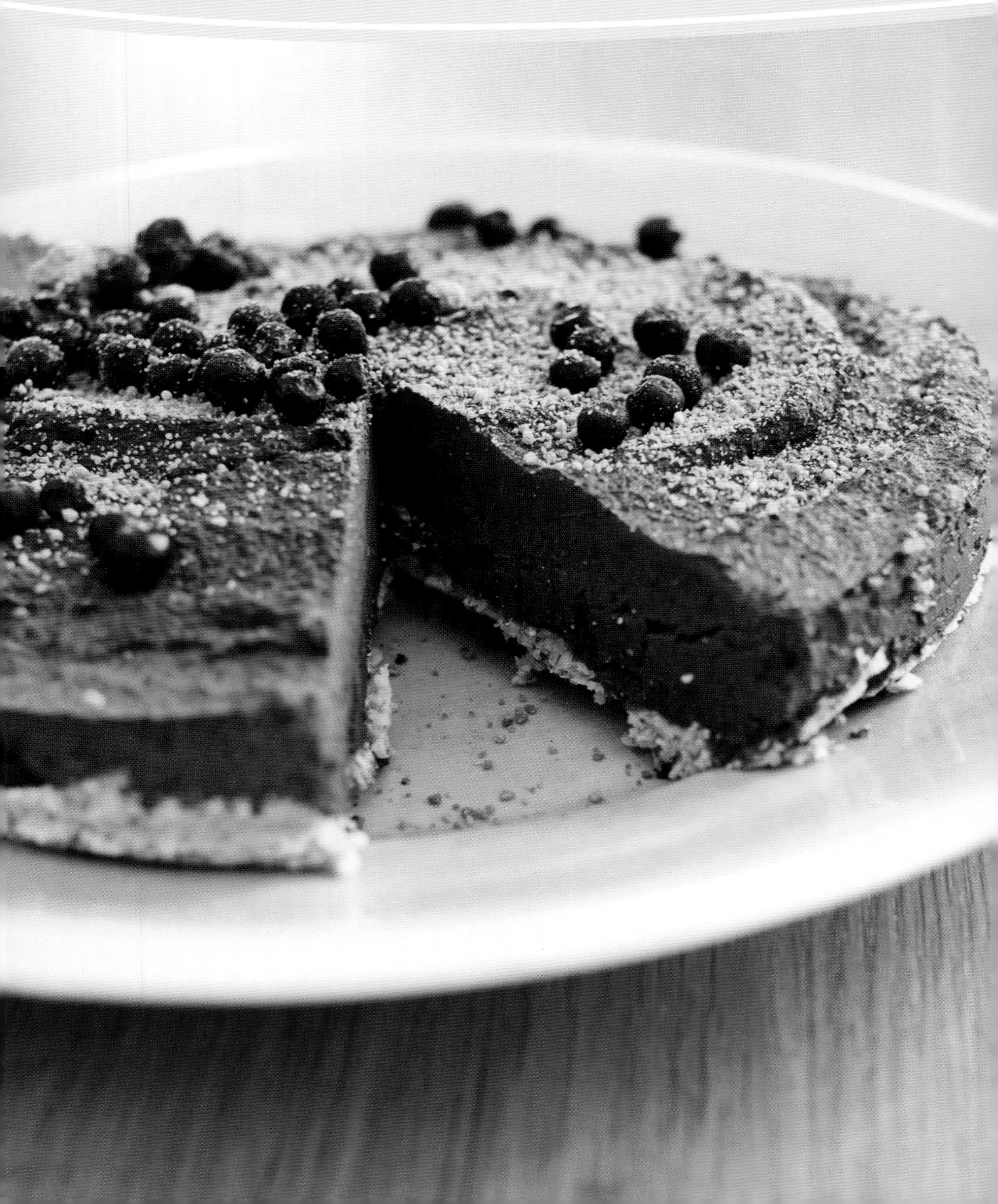

Blueberry Cheesecake

Serves: 10 / Preparation time: 20 minutes + chilling
Cooking time: 10 minutes / Calories per portion: 384

Ingredients

non-fat cooking spray

150 g / 5 oz / 1 ½ cups cashews

85 g / 3 oz / 2 cups desiccated coconut

2 tbsp coconut oil

600 g / 1 lb 5 oz / 4 cups blueberries

75 g / 3 oz / ⅓ cup light agave nectar

400 ml / 14 fl. oz / 1 ⅔ cups canned coconut
milk, chilled overnight

450 g / 1 lb / 2 cups unsweetened coconut
milk yoghurt

150 g / 5 oz / 1 cup silken tofu

Method

1. Spray the base and sides of a 20 cm
   (8 in) springform cake tin with cooking
   spray. Line the base and sides with
   greaseproof paper.

2. Pulse together 125 g / 4 oz / ¾ cup of the
   cashews with the desiccated coconut and
   coconut oil until the mixture resembles
   rough breadcrumbs. Press the mixture into
   the base of the lined tin and chill.

3. Cook together 400 g / 14 oz / 2 ⅔ cups of
   the blueberries with the agave nectar and
   2 tbsp of water in a saucepan set over a
   medium heat. Once the blueberries are soft
   and juicy, purée them in a food processor.

4. Pass the purée through a fine sieve into a
   mixing bowl. Add the chilled coconut milk,
   yoghurt and tofu, whisking until smooth.
   Scrape the mixture on top of the prepared
   base and chill for 4 hours.

5. Once set, turn out the cheesecake. Crush
   the remaining cashews and serve them as
   a garnish on top of the cheesecake, along
   with the remaining blueberries.

Snacks and Juices

Juices are a key part of any detox programme, but there are so many to choose from that it can be confusing. Many fruit juices are made from concentrate and have added sugar. Natural juices made from vegetables and other healthy ingredients can be expensive, so if you can borrow a juicer, making your own is the best option.

Caffeine may be off the menu, but herbal teas are good detoxifiers. In particular, green tea is a great choice – just check that it is caffeine-free. It has high levels of substances called catechins, which keep your liver healthy, as well as help your body produce detoxifying enzymes.

Stick to healthy options for snacking. Why not roast some chickpeas with a sprinkling of paprika or chilli powder and a drizzle of olive oil? Or make your own dips, such as hummus or green peas with mint and tahini.

Wheatgrass Banana Smoothie

Serves: 4 / Preparation time: 10 minutes
Calories per portion: 107

Ingredients

150 g / 5 oz / 3 cups wheatgrass, washed and chopped

1 l / 1 pint 16 fl. oz / 4 cups iced water

1 tbsp lemon juice

2 large bananas, chopped

2 tbsp light agave nectar

110 g / 4 oz / ½ cup crushed ice

Method

1. Combine the wheatgrass, water and lemon juice in a food processor. Blend on high for 2 minutes until evenly green and frothy.

2. Pass the liquid through a fine sieve into a jug and then back into the food processor.

3. Add the banana, agave nectar and ice. Blend on high for 1 minute until smooth.

4. Pour into glasses and serve immediately.

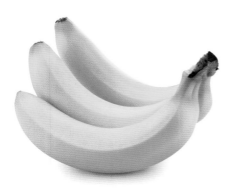

Summer Veg Rolls

Makes: 8 rolls / Preparation time: 15 minutes
Calories per portion: 59

Ingredients

2 tbsp rice wine vinegar

1 tbsp fish sauce

1 tbsp honey

1 clove of garlic, minced

½ tsp wasabi paste

110 ml / 4 fl. oz / ½ cup avocado oil

8 rice spring roll wrappers, kept under a
damp cloth

a small bunch of mint, leaves picked

75 g / 3 oz / 3 cups bean sprouts

2 large carrots, peeled and julienned

1 medium cucumber, seeded and cut into
thin batons

Method

1. Whisk together the vinegar, fish sauce,
honey, garlic and wasabi paste in a small
mixing bowl. Whisk in the avocado oil in a
slow, steady stream until emulsified. Set to
one side.

2. Working quickly one-by-one, line the centre
of each wrapper with mint leaves and top
with a mixture of the bean sprouts, carrots
and cucumber.

3. Spoon 1 tsp of the dressing on top of the
vegetables and bring the edges of the
wrappers inwards before rolling tightly.

4. Serve the rolls with the remaining dressing
on the side.

Avocado Peanut Smoothie

Serves: 4 / Preparation time: 10 minutes
Calories per portion: 194

Ingredients

750 ml / 1 pint 6 fl. oz / 3 cups unsweetened almond milk

110 g / 4 oz / ½ cup crushed ice

55 g / 2 oz / ¼ cup peanut butter

1 small cucumber, peeled and diced

1 large Hass avocado, pitted and diced

a small bunch of coriander (cilantro), leaves picked

½ lime, juiced

a pinch of salt

1 tsp red chilli (chili) powder, to garnish

Method

1. Combine the almond milk, crushed ice, peanut butter, cucumber, avocado, a handful of coriander leaves, lime juice and a pinch of salt in a food processor or blender.

2. Blend on high until smooth.

3. Pour into glasses and garnish with more coriander leaves and a pinch of chilli powder on top.

Wakame Seaweed Salad

Serves: 4 / Preparation time: 20 minutes
Calories per portion: 350

Ingredients

225 g / 8 oz / 2 cups fine rice noodles

55 ml / 2 fl. oz / ¼ cup sesame oil

75 ml / 3 fl. oz / ⅓ cup rice wine vinegar

2 tbsp tamari soy sauce

150 g / 5 oz / 3 cups wakame seaweed, shredded

2 sheets of dried seaweed, chopped

2 tbsp sesame seeds

a large handful of crispy fried rice noodles, to garnish

Method

1. Place the fine rice noodles and 1 tbsp of sesame oil in a heatproof bowl and cover with boiling water. Leave to soak for 10 minutes until soft.

2. Whisk together the remaining oil with the rice wine vinegar and soy sauce in a mixing bowl. Add the shredded and dried seaweed, tossing well to coat.

3. Once the noodles are soft, drain and add them to the seaweed, tossing well.

4. Lift the salad into bowls and top with a garnish of sesame seeds and crispy rice noodles.

Blueberry, Kiwi and Grape Smoothie

Serves: 4 / Preparation time: 10 minutes
Calories per portion: 153

Ingredients

5 kiwi fruit
350 g / 12 oz / 2 ⅓ cups frozen blueberries
300 g / 11 oz / 2 cups black seedless grapes
250 ml / 9 fl. oz / 1 cup cold sparkling water

Method

1. Slice one kiwi fruit into slices and set to one side. Peel and chop the remaining kiwi fruit.

2. Combine the chopped kiwi fruit with the blueberries, grapes and sparkling water in a food processor or blender.

3. Blend on high for 2–3 minutes until smooth.

4. Pour into glasses and serve with a slice of kiwi fruit on the rim.

Kale and Cashew Pesto

Makes: 10 servings / Preparation time: 5 minutes
Calories per portion: 104

Ingredients

110 g / 4 oz / ¾ cup cashews, toasted

2 tbsp nutritional yeast

3 cloves of garlic

175 ml / 6 fl. oz / ¾ cup avocado oil

110 g / 4 oz / 2 cups kale

1 lemon, juiced

salt and freshly ground black pepper

Method

1. Combine the cashews, nutritional yeast, garlic, oil, kale and lemon juice in a food processor and whizz to a paste.

2. Season to taste and scrape into a jar. Cover and keep in the fridge for up to one week.

Iced Courgette Smoothie

Serves: 4 / Preparation time: 10 minutes
Calories per portion: 159

Ingredients

250 ml / 9 fl. oz / 1 cup unsweetened almond milk

75 g / 3 oz / ⅓ cup unsweetened coconut milk yoghurt

750 g / 1 lb 10 oz / 6 cups courgettes (zucchinis), roughly chopped

750 ml / 1 pint 6 fl. oz / 3 cups water

a small bunch of mint

500 g / 1 lb 2 oz / 2 cups ice cubes, to serve

Method

1. Combine the almond milk, yoghurt, courgette, water and mint in a food processor or blender.

2. Blend on high until smooth.

3. Divide the ice cubes between the glasses and pour the smoothie over. Garnish with more mint leaves to serve.

Detox Chocolate Hearts

Makes: 24 hearts / Preparation time: 20 minutes + 1 hour
Cooking time: 5 minutes / Calories per portion: 76

Ingredients

2 tbsp acai berries

1 tbsp hemp seeds

110 ml / 4 fl. oz / ½ cup unsweetened coconut milk

1 tbsp wheatgrass powder

1 tbsp stevia

2 tbsp carob powder

150 g / 5 oz / 1 cup 100% raw unsweetened chocolate, chopped

3 tbsp coconut oil

3 tbsp dark agave nectar

non-fat cooking spray

Method

1. Combine the berries, hemp seeds, coconut milk, wheatgrass powder, stevia and carob powder in a food processor. Leave to soak for 10 minutes and then blend until smooth.

2. Pour into a heatproof bowl and add the chocolate, coconut oil and agave nectar. Set the bowl on top of a half-filled saucepan of gently simmering water.

3. Stir occasionally until the chocolate has melted and the mixture is smooth.

4. Spray a 24-hole heart-shaped confectionary mould with non-fat cooking spray. Pour the chocolate mixture into the moulds and chill for 1 hour until firm.

5. Once set, turn out and serve.

7-day Detox Plan

You've read the theory, you've seen the recipes – now it's time to put your detox plan into action. You'll get the best results if you plan ahead, so take the time to work out how you're going to tackle your detox.

The plans on the next few pages will give you some ideas, but feel free to adapt them if you like. For example, you may want to start with a water-only fast or keep up the juice fast for more than two days. If you do this, be aware that you may feel tired, light-headed or nauseous. It might be worth introducing food sooner than you planned if you feel unwell. Some people like to stick to raw plant-based food for the entire week; others re-introduce lean meats and fish. The choice is yours!

Planning ahead is crucial, otherwise you might have a day where you're pressed for time and don't have the right ingredients on hand. It's at times like these when you're likely to reach for what's available and break your detox rules. Shop for at least a few days' worth of meals and juices before you start and think about preparing some dishes ahead of time.

Your detox programme will be easier to stick to if you don't have a big blow-out the night before you start. Instead, gradually reduce your intake of caffeine, alcohol, nicotine and sugar in the week before your detox starts. This will make it less challenging than going cold-turkey.

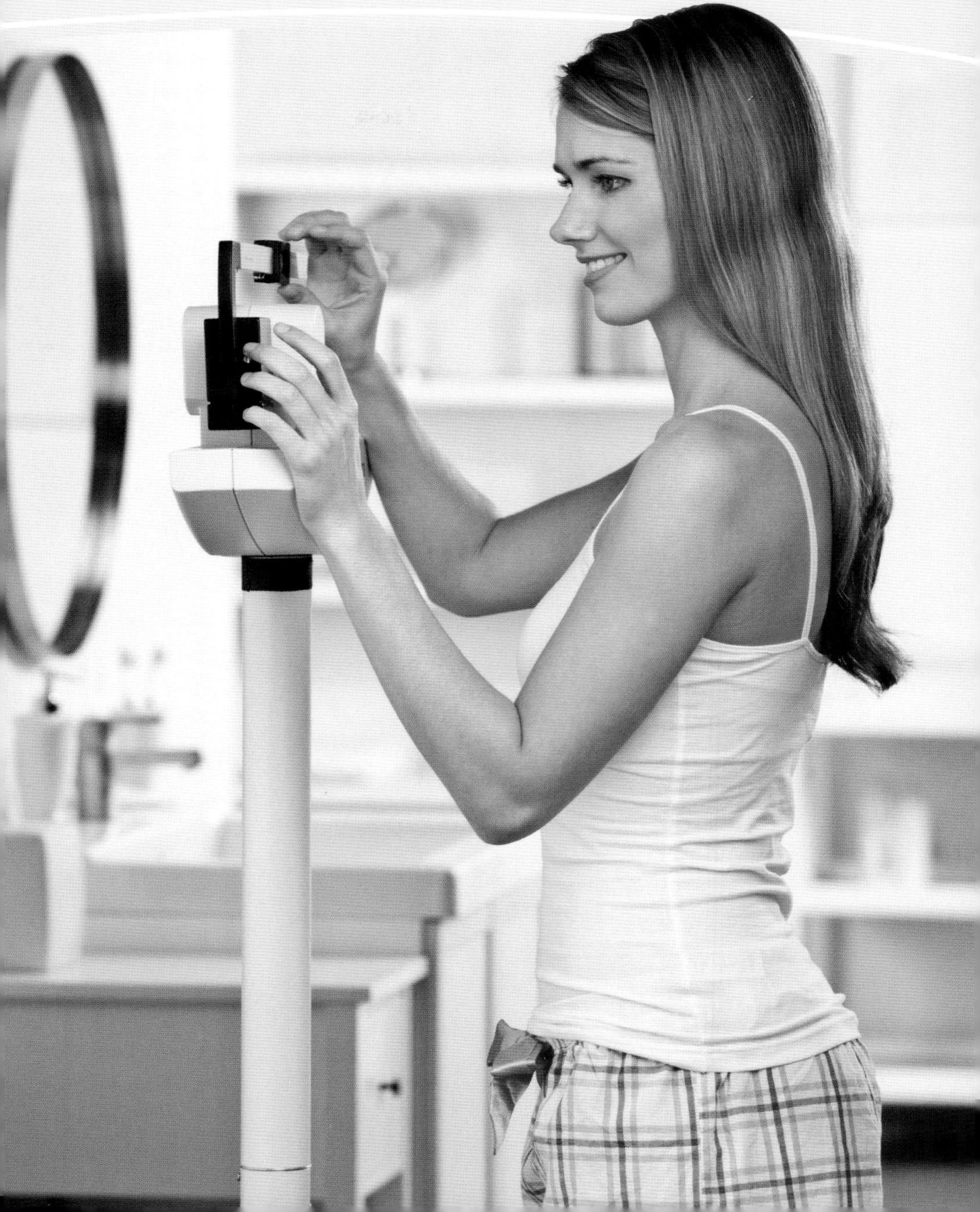

Days 1 and 2

You may want to start your detox with a juice fast. Aim to have around four 200–250 ml glasses of juice and about eight 200 ml glasses of water per day.

Starting weight

Day 1	Ingredients	Amount
Juice 1		
Juice 2		
Juice 3		
Juice 4		

Amount of water drunk:	
Activity log:	
Hours of sleep:	
How I feel:	

Reward for hitting my target:	

Day 2	Ingredients	Amount
Juice 1		
Juice 2		
Juice 3		
Juice 4		

Amount of water drunk:	
Activity log:	
Hours of sleep:	
How I feel:	
Reward for hitting my target:	

Days 3 and 4

Now may be the time to re-introduce some healthy foods. Stick to plant-based food as much as possible, eat it raw or lightly steamed and keep portions on the small side. Don't forget to keep drinking water!

Day 3	Food	Drink
Breakfast		
Lunch		
Snack		
Dinner		

Amount of water drunk:	
Activity log:	
Hours of sleep:	
How I feel:	
Reward for hitting my target:	

Day 4	Food	Drink
Breakfast		
Lunch		
Snack		
Dinner		

Amount of water drunk:	
Activity log:	
Hours of sleep:	
How I feel:	
Reward for hitting my target:	

Days 5 and 6

Now that you're well into your detox, you may want to add lean meat and fish to your diet. Don't let it take over, though – keep the main focus on vegetables, legumes, fruits, nuts and seeds.

Day 5	Food	Drink
Breakfast		
Lunch		
Snack		
Dinner		

Amount of water drunk:	
Activity log:	
Hours of sleep:	
How I feel:	
Reward for hitting my target:	

Day 6	Food	Drink
Breakfast		
Lunch		
Snack		
Dinner		

Amount of water drunk:	
Activity log:	
Hours of sleep:	
How I feel:	
Reward for hitting my target:	

Day 7 and Notes

Nearly there! Just one more day to go and you should already be feeling the positive effects of your detox. Keep it up – your body will thank you!

Day 7	Food	Drink
Breakfast		
Lunch		
Snack		
Dinner		

Amount of water drunk:	
Activity log:	
Hours of sleep:	
How I feel:	
Reward for hitting my target:	

Detox review

When you've finished your detox, jot down a few notes about its best points, as well as the biggest challenges. Did you see any correlations between what you ate and drank and how you felt? Next time you're ready for a detox, you can look back through these notes to help plan the best possible week.

Finishing weight

Juices – what worked and what didn't:

Best new recipes:

New ingredients:

Energy levels:

Meditation tips:

Positive effects:

Side effects:

Shopping List

When planning a detox, it's good to make sure that your kitchen is stocked up with the essentials before you start. You'll be making regular trips to the supermarket or farmers' market to buy fresh fruit and veg, but there are less-perishable ingredients that are always good to have on hand. Here are a few suggestions for what to put on your shopping list.

Grains and pulses

brown rice

buckwheat

chickpeas (garbanzo beans)

kidney beans

lentils

oats

quinoa

wholegrain pasta

Cooking essentials

avocado oil

coconut oil

dried herbs

extra-virgin olive oil

flaxseed oil

hempseed oil

mustard

salt and pepper

spices

tahini paste

nut butter

Snacks

almonds

cashews

chia seeds

dried fruit (unsulphured)

flaxseeds

hemp seeds

pecans

pumpkin seeds

sunflower seeds

walnuts

wholegrain crackers

Everyday Detox

Once your detox is finished, you want to keep feeling the benefits. If you slip right back into your old unhealthy diet, all the good work you did during the detox will be wasted. Try to work the basic detox principles into your everyday life. You don't necessarily need to fast regularly, but take a good hard look at your diet and see where you could make long-term changes that will have a positive impact on your health and well-being. The chart on the right will give you some ideas.

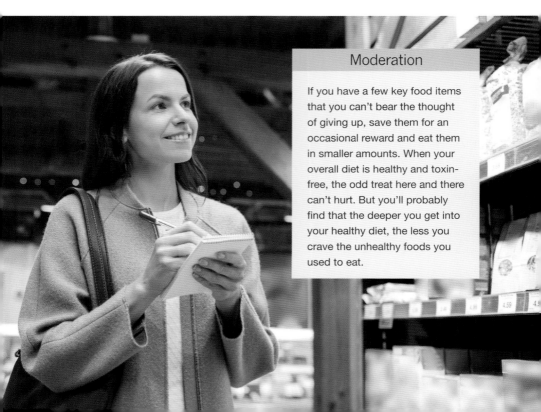

Moderation

If you have a few key food items that you can't bear the thought of giving up, save them for an occasional reward and eat them in smaller amounts. When your overall diet is healthy and toxin-free, the odd treat here and there can't hurt. But you'll probably find that the deeper you get into your healthy diet, the less you crave the unhealthy foods you used to eat.

Get rid of...	...and replace it with:
battered fish	baked or grilled fish
beef mince	turkey mince or vegetarian mince
biscuits	oatcakes and rice cakes
Cheddar cheese	reduced-fat cheese or naturally low-fat cheeses such as cottage cheese
creamy or cheesy sauces	tomato or vegetable-based sauces
crisps	nuts, seeds, dried fruit or roasted chickpeas (garbanzo beans)
flour tortillas	corn tortillas
fried chicken	roasted or grilled chicken breast
jam or other sugary spreads	low-fat cream cheese, mashed avocado or jams sweetened with natural fruit extract
table salt	fresh herbs and spices
semi-skimmed or whole milk	skimmed milk, almond milk or soya milk
sugary breakfast cereal	wholegrain cereal or home-made porridge and granola
sugary fizzy drinks	water, or a small amount of fruit juice mixed with sparkling water
vegetable oils such as sunflower oil, rapeseed oil, corn oil, etc	olive oil, flaxseed oil, hempseed oil, coconut oil, avocado oil
white bread, crumpets or muffins	wholegrain or gluten-free equivalents
white rice (basmati, long grain, etc)	brown rice
white sugar	maple syrup, coconut sugar, agave nectar, honey or stevia

Toxin-free Lifestyle

Detox is more than just a week-long challenge – it's a lifestyle choice and ridding your diet of unhealthy foods is just the start. A detox lifestyle is all about making informed choices about the foods we eat and the products we use. Aiming for the most natural, toxin-free life will have incredible health benefits.

Clean cosmetics

Read the labels on the products you use on your body – many cosmetics and hair products are loaded with chemicals and toxins. Organic brands are available, and some manufacturers make sure that their products are free of parabens, phthalates, nano-particles and other nasties. You can also make your own natural products – the internet is full of recipes and ideas.

Clean up your cleaning

Not only do many cleaning products contain toxins that can harm your body, they are also bad for the environment. However, if you do your research, you'll find eco-friendly alternatives that are kinder to your body, too. You'll be surprised at how much you can do with inexpensive natural products such as bicarbonate of soda, vinegar, lemon juice and olive oil. Use essential oils such as lavender, peppermint, eucalyptus, lemon grass or tea tree oil to keep your home smelling fresh and fragrant.

Cut the stress!

Detox isn't just about the tangible things we put on or in our bodies.
Stress can also have a negative effect on health, so try to cut it out of your
life as much as possible. Try to eliminate the causes of stress in your life,
such as unhealthy relationships, and use meditation as a way of dealing with
the ones you can't escape. Making regular time for meditation can help keep
your mind and body in balance.

Diet consultant: Jo Stimpson

Written by: Ruth Manning

Main food photography and recipe development:
© Stockfood, The Food Media Agency

Picture Credits:
Dreamstime: Wavebreakmedia 4, Citalliance 6,
Dmitry Kalinovsky 8, Boggy 11, Nyul 12, Monkey
Business Images 13, 25, Martinmark 15, Anna
Kucherova 17, Serhiy Shullye 28, Hannu Viitanen
31, Benoit Daoust 39, Valentina Razumova 44,
Werner Münzker 48, David Franklin 51, Petr Goskov
52, Vitaly Mikhaylov 56, Peter Zijlstra 60, Svetlana
Kuznetsova 63, Harald Biebel 64, Agorulko 67,
Sommai Sommai 68, Vitalii Hrytsiv 71, Yurakp
72, Ovydyborets 78, Valentyn75 81, Melica 123,
Syda Productions 124; Shutterstock: Maridav 9,
Everything 10, Elena Elisseeva 11tr, Pressmaster
16, LuckyImages 19, Luminaimages 20, Monkey
Business Images 22, 122, Mr. Suttipon Yakham
32, Olga Miltsova 35, Viktar Malyshchyts 36, Iurii
Kachkovskyi 40, Binh Thanh Bui 47, 107, Maks
Narodenko 55, Mareandmare 75, Africa Studio
82, D7INAMI7S 85, Nataliia Melnychuk 86, Maks
Narodenko 89, Miguel Garcia Saavedra 90, Nata-
Lia 93, Maks Narodenko 96, Yasonya 99, Anna
Kucherova 100, ComZeal 103, Kostiantyn Fastov
104, Valentyn Volkov 108, Valentina Razumova 111,
AVAVA 113, Verca 115, Volosina 117l, Igor Dutina
119, Racorn 127, Rido 128.